Think Like a Winner!

Unlocking the Power Inside You

By Anthony M. Fourshee

Copyright © 2016 Anthony M Fourshee. All Rights Reserved

Contents

Introduction	4
Chapter 1: The Start of Defeat	6
Chapter 2: The Shift in Change!	12
Chapter 3: Identity Crisis	16
Chapter 4: Finding My Niche	22
Chapter 5: Taking Off the Mask	26
Chapter 6: It's a Pleasure to Meet You!	33
Chapter 7: And the Journey Begins	39
Chapter 8: Vocalizing Your Victory	46
Chapter 9: Go with Your Gut!	51

Chapter 10: There Is a War!   58

Chapter 11: Hitting the Road   62

Chapter 12: This Girl Gets Me!   68

Chapter 13: The Power of Purpose   72

Chapter 14: Obstacles Will Come   76

Chapter 15: You Are Not Alone   81

Chapter 16: Tired of Being Sick and Tired   85

Chapter 17: No Pain, No Gain   89

Chapter 18: FEAR   93

Chapter 19: Fatherhood   102

Chapter 20: Be Healed!!   108

Introduction

This book is about an incredibly amazing journey that God has allowed me to be a character in. It's an exploration of discovering how God's power is released in His love for us. I pray that my experiences ignite a burning passion for you to be magnetized by His love.

Do you feel like you're losing in life? Have you ever felt like nothing goes your way, or you're always coming in last? People today are struggling to get by, simply coasting through life, yielding at life's green light as if it were red, and just, throwing in the towel before they even get in the ring. Hope seems to be an extinct, four-letter word that has sailed off into the distant sunset. Where is peace? Where is joy? Has it been stolen from us and looted like one- legged pirates searching for treasure, taking our ships captive and ransoming us off as if we were cattle?

I realize that for many people, this is their personal reality, but it doesn't have to be. You can live a blessed and prosperous life. You can live a life full of joy, peace and purpose. Yes! This is possible, if you think like a winner and unlock the power inside of you.

Chapter 1

The Start of Defeat

"Defeat is only the end when you have no pulse left!"

~**Anthony M. Fourshee**

The funny thing about life is that it never quite measures up to what you expect it to be. When I was younger, I imagined that I would be able to do something that was extraordinary. But, the funny thing is, I didn't know what it was that I would do. I didn't even know how to define extraordinary. But life has a way of giving you on-the-job training. Life teaches you as you go along. But the key is to listen and learn from life. Learn from situations, trials, failures and even success.

The truth is, most of the time we forget to take time and really take inventory of our situation and circumstance. We tend to be discipled by the "school of hard knocks." Learning this way creates a defeated mindset. It's a mindset that we take on and don't even realize that we have taken on. You see, it's hard to see yourself as a winner with a defeated mindset. A defeated mindset highlights why you *can't* do something rather than why you *can*. A defeated mindset focuses on failure rather than success. A defeated mindset is excuse driven." I can't do this because. . ." "I know but . . ." or "If only I had . . ."

How many times have you used these excuses? Probably more than you can even count. I know I have. I believe these phrases were the driving force of my quick-to-quit behavior. My quick to quit behavior started when I was just a kid. You see, I was a heavy kid, and growing up in the 80s most kids really got singled out for being heavy. It wasn't like nowadays when you have an overabundance of overweight kids in classrooms. I was in my own little world with my best friend Curt.

I grew up in Trenton, New Jersey with my older brother Ameil, who was, in my opinion, the coolest kid in the world! And I say that not just because he was my brother--he really was. I mean, my brother had everything going for him. He was smart, good looking and tough. No one would mess with him because he was an expert martial artist. My father owned a karate school, so my brother trained all the time.

I remember one time, I was getting teased and bullied by these 4 teenagers. I was only about seven years old, and these guys were all about 14 to 15 years old. The leader of the group picked me up and began to slam me against a brick wall in front of our neighbor's house. I remember being so scared. Water was pouring out of my eyes; when out of nowhere comes my brother to the rescue! It was just like something out of a movie! I remember my brother telling him, "Put him down before I break your nose!" The kid threw me down to the ground and threw a punch at my brother. Before you knew it, my brother's foot was clean on the kid's nose. His nose erupted like a volcano, sending blood everywhere! I never saw that much blood gush out of anyone's nose before. The other 3 ran down the street to go get help. They quickly came back with the kid's older brother and sister, and they both had bats. I remember my brother taking them out as if he was Bruce Lee himself. It was a scene straight out of Hollywood. My brother even kept the bats. I guess they were his trophies.

After that incident, my parents moved our family from the city to the suburbs. I was 8 and my brother was 16. This was very hard for me, because it meant that I would be leaving my best friend Curt. Growing up in the city, I didn't really think that I understood that I was different from other kids.

Curt never brought up my weight. To him and my family, it really didn't seem to make much of a difference that I was overweight-- until that day Ameil saved me. That day changed my life; but it changed for the worst. You see, I began to view my life through defeated lenses. I never felt good about myself. I never had the confidence to see anything through or to finish anything. I was quick to quit anything that required work. After we moved, I started going to an elementary school in the suburbs. I was so intimidated by the kids there. I was the new kid, the only heavy kid, and my self-worth was still hanging on that brick wall that teenager slammed me against.

My morale was so low, and my first day of school didn't help either. All of the kids stared at me in class as if I were some freak of nature. I had a tough time adjusting. On the first day of school, my new teacher asked me to stand up and introduce myself to the class--talk about fear! I was totally paralyzed! I could not move. I just sat there with my eyes clinched close, hoping she would move on to someone else. She called me three times, and, of course, I did not respond. By now every student in the class was laughing at me. Now, not only was I the fattest kid in the 3rd grade, but I was also the dumbest kid. At least that's what I thought they were thinking. As the school year went on, I developed a fear of reading. I think this was because the teacher would call on me to read out loud in front of the class.

My mindset was so defeated. I could not make any new friends. Food became my comfort even more. I was so terrified of being noticed. I would refuse to read anything out loud or go to the chalkboard for math problems. This affected my learning to the point that the principle was considering keeping me in the 3rd grade another year.

I believe that everyone has several milestones in their lives. These milestones are forks in the road of life where a simple decision can change your life for the better, or the worse. I believe this was my first milestone. But God had a plan. My mother and my Aunt both recognized this landmark in my life. You see, they knew that the trouble I was having wasn't my inability to learn, it was my lack of confidence that was having an effect on my learning. They knew that the root of the problem my weight. And if I was to stay back a year, the kids would be smaller, and I would be bigger, and more teasing would occur. So they both went to the principle to fight for me. He agreed that if I passed a 4th grade placement test before the school year started, then I could advance to the 4th grade. But if I failed, I would return to the 3rd grade. My parents hired my teacher to tutor me one-on-one over the summer. This [obscured] start shifting the change in my life [obscured]

•Ti[p obscured]

Nev[er obscured] [jud]gements define who you are.
Let [obscured] [umb]rella. And watch the
judge[ments obscured] [um]brella like rain drops.

Chapter 2

A Shift in Change!

"Change is a choice! So choose to change before change chooses you!"

~Anthony M. Fourshee

A week after school ended I started tutoring with Mrs. Marilyn Bell-Di Lascio. I really didn't know what to expect. Mrs. DiLascio was a soft- spoken Canadian woman who always smelled nice. She wasn't a mean teacher; however she never allowed any of the kids to pull one over on her. As my mother and I pulled up in front of Mrs. DiLascio's house for our first session, my stomach was twisted up like a soft Philly pretzel. My hands were wet and shriveled up like a restaurant pot washer. My mouth was so dry, if I would have spoken, a tumble weed probably would have fallen out. As I walked up the driveway, I was amazed by the many brilliant colors illuminating from the flowers of her magnificently manicured garden. I rang the doorbell not knowing what to expect, when suddenly the door opened up with Mrs. DiLascio greeting me with the biggest smile. Her smile was so infectious, as if she were a completely different person. She was so excited to see me. It had only been a week since I had last seen her, but it didn't seem like that to her. She gave me an enormously huge hug, which put a hefty smile on my face. She invited me in and immediately my nose was overtaken with the smell of chocolate chip cookies. This was the ultimate ice breaker. Any nervousness I had vanished at the smell of those cookies. All we did that first session was bake cookies. I didn't realize that she was teaching me without me knowing she was teaching me. You see, she was showing me how to measure and how to use the measurement system. I outright had a blast that day! She constantly rewarded me with hugs and told me how well I was doing. This day was the first step in learning how to believe in myself. The more Mrs. DiLascio affirmed me, the more confidence I began to have in myself. Because of her tutoring, I passed the exam with flying colors and was able to advance to the 4th grade!

    That summer changed my life! She created an environment that cultivated success. You see, greatness was already inside of me, it just needed to be recognized and nurtured in me, just like greatness is inside of you! Maybe you never had a Mrs. DiLascio in your life. Maybe nobody ever told you how special you are, or that you can accomplish a goal. Well I'm telling you that you are! You have the potential to do great things, if you shift your thinking. I wasn't born looking through defeated lenses. My vision got blurry from trauma, and I made the choice to put those lenses on myself. Like me, maybe you have experienced an unbearable trauma in your childhood, and this trauma has locked up the winner inside of you. Make the decision today to put on new lenses. Ask God to remove and heal you from the trauma, and believe that He has. Even if you feel like nothing has changed. Trust me it has, because you are planting fresh seeds of victory. When a farmer plants his seeds, they don't grow into a crop overnight. He plants them by faith and he knows that there are some things he has to do to nurture those seeds to receive his crops--like water and fertilize it. But he can't see under the ground; so how does he know if his seeds are going to grow?

-- by faith. And by faith you are a winner, even if you don't feel like it.

•Tips for the Winner•

Never let the fear of life changes stop you from moving forward. Look at life changes as a piggy bank. Every change you put in the bank adds up. And in time, before you know it, you have a little nest egg saved; just like every change in life adds up, expanding your experience.

Chapter 3

Identity Crisis

"If you find your identity, there is no crisis!"

~Anthony M. Fourshee

Throughout my lower-school years, my parents weren't really around as much as I would have liked. My father was a remarkable salesman for one of the largest lightbulb manufactures in the U.S. In fact, he was the first and only African American employee in the corporate office. He started out as a truck driver with no high school diploma. He worked his way up to be one of the top grossing salesmen in his office, with millions of dollars in sales. My mother worked as a porter in a well-known pharmaceutical company. She worked nights, so I only saw her on the weekends--that is, if she didn't work overtime. My dad, however, I never saw. He was always on the road. His only day home--which was on Sunday--was spent in front of the television watching football all day. So I was practically raised by my big brother, Ameil. This was fine by me, because I looked up to him so much. We weren't rich, but my parents made great money. So we didn't have any worry of lack. For a 17- year-old, my brother was very influential. He had an amazing effect on people. Ameil was very popular. His reputation was legendary. All the ladies wanted to be with him. All the fellas wanted to be him. My brother was like a celebrity in our town. Everyone knew his name. And he took me everywhere with him. I was like one of his entourage--well, more like a mascot, but I was enjoying the ride! But this had an upside and a downside. On the upside, at 10 years old, I got to go to all of the cool high school parties and hangout with all the pretty girls. I was always being told how cute I was by them--in a mascot kind of way. On the downside, I was being exposed to alcohol, drugs, sex and pornography. Now, don't get me wrong, my brother never allowed me to participate in any of those things. However, I saw them first hand with my own eyes. Being exposed to these things at 10 years old has a traumatic impact on one's identity, especially when there's no explanation as to what's going on or what I was seeing. I never asked questions. I just ran everything through my 10-year-old filter and came up with my own level of understanding. So I adapted and developed a chameleon spirit, meaning, I adjusted to whatever the situation that was going on in my life. I would be whatever anyone wanted me to be in order for them to like me. I was still dealing with my weight issues, and this gave me an additional reason to desire man's approval. I, like so many other kids in my situation, was forced to grow up too soon and missed out on just being a kid.

For many years I was a silent, secret student of my brother. He was my secret sensei. But what Ameil was unknowingly teaching me had nothing to do with the martial arts he was so well trained in. I was learning how to be the life of the party. I realized that if I got everyone to laugh *with* me, they wouldn't laugh *at* me. I learned how to charm the ladies so they would look passed my weight. I was determined not to feel any pain anymore. I was determined to be popular. I was determined to be cool. I was going to do whatever it took to find my niche that would allow me to stand out and be noticed in a positive way.

I developed a love for dancing, I guess because of all the parties I went to with my brother. I would dance all the time. It didn't matter where I was or who was watching. When I was 12, I developed a friendship with a guy by the name of Sim. Sim was an extremely talented guy. He could sing, dance, rap--and he was very good looking. He was one of those guys that didn't have to have a niche, because he was the full package. He reminded me a lot of my brother. I guess that's why we became such good friends. Sim was a grade ahead of me, so by the time I got to high school he was already the popular one, and I was just his side-kick friend. But this would all change at my first high school dance.

It was 3 weeks into my freshman year. I recall ironing the creases down the middle of my Lee jeans. I loved to feel the warmth on my legs as I put them on. Then, I' slid my "ANTHONY" name plate belt buckle on, and finished it all up with my blue suede, Puma sneakers. As soon as Sim and I walked into that dance, all eyes were on us. Well, all eyes were on Sim. (Remember, I was just his side kick at that time.) Sim asked someone to dance and was on the dance floor enjoying himself. And where was I? --being a wall flower, of course.

Remember when I previously mentioned that we all have several milestones in our lives--forks in the road of life where a simple decision can change your life for the better, or the worse? I believe this was my second milestone. I took a look at the dance floor and it was as if God had slowed down time. I could see how everyone was smiling and enjoying themselves. It was as if I could somehow feel their emotions. Joy began to rise up in me. Then, I slowly looked at the people who were to the left and right of me, standing up against the wall. And again I could feel their emotions. I immediately began to feel sad, alone and abandoned. Thoughts of being slammed against that brick wall when I was a kid flew through my mind. I could literally see in my mind, one of those planes in advertisements that fly over the beaches. But instead of the sign reading "amusement rides at the steel pier" it read, "Take a chance!" This jumped in my spirit! Boldness came upon me! This was my pivotal moment. And what I did next would drop the jaws of many.

•Tips for the Winner•

Whether you had a great childhood, or a not-so-great childhood, use the good and the bad as fuel to drive you to your destiny.

Chapter 4

Finding My Niche

"God's love for us is incomprehensible to the human mind, without the Holy Spirit's guidance!"

~Anthony M. Fourshee

Even though I didn't personally know God yet at that dance, He knew me. I understand now that what I was experiencing was a vision, and God was communicating with me. He had given me an opportunity to be courageous, and I was going to seize that opportunity.

I went on a search to find Jennifer. Jennifer was the finest and most popular senior in school. I figured that if everyone saw me, a freshman, dancing with her, a senior, my reputation would be massive. I spotted Jennifer over by the DJ booth with a group of girls. My eyes were locked in on her like a sniper on his target. So

I started my approach. My heart was pounding. My hands were shaking. With each step I took, my legs would get weaker and weaker. But I was determined not to give up. No one knew what I was doing, so I could have bailed at any moment. But I couldn't bail; I knew somehow in my gut that I was going to make my mark at that dance. And that was my only option. As I approached her, she turned around, and with her light brown eyes gazing towards me, she offered up this enticing smile. I thought to myself, "She's checking me out!" With a spring in her step, she immediately began to jog towards me with her arms open wide. I couldn't believe it! This was a dream come true! But unfortunately she ran right by me and hugged the guy that was walking behind me. Talk about embarrassing! Thank goodness nobody knew what I was getting ready to do. I played it off pretty smoothly, but my heart was filled with disappointment. I sat there for about ten minutes. Sim was still on the dance floor enjoying himself. And that was the exact place I wanted to be. Sometimes in life, what you expect to be your breakthrough won't be; but what you least expect will be.

I received a tap on my shoulder. And when I looked up, I was greeted by a friendly familiar face. It was Yolanda. Yolanda was a good friend of ours who lived up the street. She was a junior, and one of the coolest people to hang out with. She asked me to dance and, of course, I said yes. Dancing with Yolanda came with no pressure. I wasn't worried about my reputation or being popular. But something happened to me on that dance floor. I had this supernatural sensation come over me. I began to do moves that I had never done before. My passion for dancing intensified as the bass of the music pounded on the ears of my heart. The melodies took control of my body and directed it like a conductor. By now, crowds began to form around us. Everyone else stopped dancing to observe the phenomenon that was taking place. Yolanda stopped dancing, but Sim came over in the circle with me. The dance floor was ours. Everyone was amazed! No one had ever seen a big guy like me move like that before. Everyone was talking about it. From that point on, I began to dance anywhere at any time. I found my niche. Everyone knew my name now. I was popular. And now all my problems would be solved--or so I thought! God supernaturally anointed me that day for a purpose that it would take me three years to discover.

•Tips for the Winner•

What is it the separates you from the crowd? What's your niche? You have inside of you something that no other human being has. The key is to discover what is and effectively utilize it to stand out.

Chapter 5

Taking Off the Mask

"Halloween is once a year, but we tend to wear a mask every day!"

~ Anthony M. Fourshee

By the time I was a junior, I had accomplished everything I said I was going to accomplish. I was popular. Everyone liked me. I had influence in my school. I did everything I thought I needed to do to be a winner. I became who I thought I needed to become to be a winner. But something still troubled me, and I didn't understand what it was. I didn't feel like a winner. And I sure wasn't thinking like a winner. One day, I woke up and asked myself," what is it that I'm trying to win? Who was I trying to please?" I had so many people around me, yet, I felt so all alone. I felt as if my heart had been covered in thick, black oil that tucked itself away in a deep, dark abandoned cave of isolation.

This was really troubling me. However, I just suppressed it and put on the mask I created. Putting on the mask was exhausting! Talk about high maintenance! Having to say the right jokes at the right time, having to smile and laugh when I felt like balling my eyes out. Everyone around me saw this happy, funny, charming, amazing dancer, but I was lonely, isolated and despondent. But my third milestone was just around the corner. When I was a freshman, all students were required to take an elective. Some took auto shop, most of the girls took cosmetology, but I took food service. Well, it's no secret that I love to eat. But I'm sure you figured that out by now. In my junior year, I had Food Service class for 4 periods, which took practically the whole day. So we spent a lot of time there. Every day between classes, I would take samples of my baking to all the girls in cosmetology next door. All of the popular girls were in Cosmetology. Most of them were pretty superficial. But at that age, who cared about that? The guys in my Food Service class would beg to go with me every day. You see, the guys weren't very popular and those girls wouldn't give those guys the time of day. The only thing that moved those girls was status and pastries. I knew all the girls, so I would take a couple of the guys with me over there along with the pastries. Off course, I did all the talking. The guys would be so intimidated. They would never speak. They would just stand there and smile, while I laughed, joked and flirted with the girls. When we would leave, the guys would be so excited. I mean they'd be jumping up and down as if they got a phone number or even spoke to the girls for that matter. I was always the last one to leave. One particular day as I was leaving the Cosmetology class, I was overtaken by an overwhelming feeling of darkness. I felt a vast, loathsome desolation. I was walking in a zombie-like state when I heard a voice say, "Are you alright?" Immediately what I was feeling left at the sound of his voice. I gazed ahead to find John standing in front of me. His voice resonated concern, and his face released compassion. John was a senior. He was well known by everyone, very popular and dressed really nice. He was a really cool guy. But there was something different about him. It was as if his presence commanded respect. He was one of those people that you had to like--one of those people that you're just drawn to. This was the first time I ever encountered someone with favor. At the time I didn't know or understand what it was, but I was drawn to it. Favor is a supernatural favoritism from God. It means gaining approval, acceptance, special benefits or blessings. Whatever it was that was on John took away the darkness that was around me. After school, normally I caught a ride with one of my friends. Most of my friends were seniors and drove to school. But that day I decided to walk. As I was walking a car pulled up alongside me and rolled down the window. "Are you ok?" echoed from the car. It was John! "Yeah, man," I replied. "You want are ride?" John countered. "Sure," I replied. I got into the back seat. John's girlfriend was in the front seat. He told me that he was going to drop his girlfriend off first because she lived further away. John lived around the corner from me. I had seen him around, but I never really met or knew him. As I sat in the back seat, I felt safe. I mean, even though I didn't really know John, I felt like I didn't have to impress him. We dropped his girlfriend off and headed home. He asked if I wanted to listen to the radio and I said yes. Everyone who I hung around either listened to rap or house music. But John put on gospel music. Now the only gospel music I had ever heard was at my grandmother's house when I was younger and would go to visit her. She would put on these boring, depressing songs about coming up on the rough side of the mountain. But this music wasn't like that. It wasn't my thing, but it wasn't too bad either. As we pulled up to my house, for the first time in a long time I felt good. It was like I didn't understand what was going on around me, so I couldn't explain what I was actually feeling. All I know is I felt good.

John asked me if I needed a ride to school. I told him no because my mom usually took me to school. It's really the only time we spent together. So he said, "I'll see you around." When I woke up the next morning I had a spring in my step and a glide in my stride! Looking back, I realize that it was the Holy Spirit gradually revealing Himself to me. He was slowly releasing realms of faith. And in those realms, darkness can \not exist. That's why I felt so much peace, because all demonic principalities had fled. Every day that week, Johnny brought me home. We had gotten pretty close pretty fast. He invited me to come over to his house to chill out on Saturday. He told me that his mother and sister were going to Philly to visit his grandmother. He said that they shouldn't be back until after 6 pm. John was excited about having a women-free zone for at least a few hours.

John lived with his mother and younger sister. He also had an older sister who had 2 girls and a boy. She had her own place but practically lived with them. I arrived at his house around 10:30 and we had a blast. We joked and laughed for hours, like two little kids. We had an amazing connection. It was as if we had been friends for years. John's mom came home around 6:30. As she came in, he immediately got up to go greet her. She came and they embraced each other with the longest hug. It was as if they hadn't seen each other in years. I had never seen anything like that before. My family was not very affectionate. There were no hugs, kisses, or" I love you's." With excitement, he introduced me to his mom. I said hello and she immediately embraced me the same way she embraced him. I was wrecked! I was hit by a love I never encountered before. My body felt like it was melting. She began to pray for me in this weird language. I was not prepared for this! All I could think about was "Who was this lady? What kind of spell did she put on me? What is this presence I am feeling? I could not control my body or even talk; but I never felt so loved before. The closest I had gotten to this feeling was when Mrs. DiLascio hugged me. I began to weep uncontrollably. I was not in charge of my emotions anymore. That mask I had created had been ripped right off. With my head in her lap, she began to sing in this weird language as she slowly stroked my head. It was absolutely a divine experience.

•Tips for the Winner•

Sometimes in life, we must let down our guard and be open to receive love. I know it can be hard to trust people sometimes, especially when we have been wounded. But you can't climb to a new level in life with luggage. So let the luggage go, and free up those hands to go to another level.

Chapter 6

It's a Pleasure to Meet You!

"God loves you because He loves you--period! He loves you not because of what you do or don't do. He loves you because of what His Son did on the cross."

~Anthony M. Fourshee

    The next day, John's mom invited me to go to dinner with them after church. John and his mother went to different churches. John was a musician. He played the bass for the largest church in our town. I'm not sure why the rest of the family didn't go with him, but I don't think his mom was very fond of that church. John stopped by to pick me up. I invited him in to meet my parents. Believe it or not I was still vibrating from that run-in with his mom. John charmed my mom, and connected with my dad, which was amazing because my dad hated all of my friends. As soon as we got in the car I blurted out, "What did your mom do to me yesterday?" He began to laugh. I yelled, "It's not funny." We both looked at each other and busted out laughing. John started making these weird faces that he said I was making, as we both grabbed our stomachs to sooth the gut-wrenching pain from laughter. After we'd calmed down from the excitement, I said to him, "Seriously man, what was all of that yesterday? What did your mom do to me? Was that voodoo or something? What was that language was she speaking?" John took a deep breath, smiled and said, "Why don't you ask her yourself," as we pulled into his driveway. Off course, his mom had pulled up just before we did and was getting out of the car as we pulled up. John got out and gave his mom another one of those hugs. I stayed on the other side of the car. I wasn't falling for the hug trap again. I had no idea what was going on. But I knew it was good. I felt like I needed them. Call me crazy, but I sensed that they needed me too--or at least Johnny did. When we got to Friendly's, I just had to find out what all of that was. So I asked. I said, "I got a question." She asked, "What is it sweetheart," in an amazingly soft tone. She leaned forward as her eyes intently focused on me, as if the only thing in the world that mattered was what I had to ask her. "What happened yesterday?" She sat back in her seat, smiled and began to speak as she stirred her coffee. "The Holy Spirit wanted to introduce Himself to you." She said it just as calm. I quickly looked over at Johnny, and he shrugged his shoulders and said, "I guess He wants to use you!"

"Exactly, "exclaimed Johnny's mom" I immediately thought back to when I went to church at Easter with my grandmother. I remember them saying something about him giving up the Holy Spirit when he died. So in a panic I screamed out, "Am I going to die?" Everyone in Friendly's looked at me like I was crazy. John, his mom and little sister busted out laughing. "No silly," she said, The Holy Spirit wanted to meet you because He has big plans for you. He wants to take away all of that hurt and pain you are feeling.

He has already started taking it away. That's what was happening yesterday," She paused as she took another sip of coffee. Then she said, "On my way home, The Lord told me that Johnny's new friend needs to be loved. And that's why I embraced you. That language I was speaking in was my spiritual language. Some people call it praying in tongues! And the vibrations you were feeling was the power of God running through your body." I began to feel so appreciated, so valued. I started thinking to myself, "Why would someone who doesn't even know me talk to God who doesn't care about me." Johnny's mom smiled and said, "Because He loves you!" Now

Think Like A Winner! *Unlocking the Power Inside You*

this really freaked me out! It was as if she knew exactly what I was thinking. I was so confused. I didn't say another word that night. I just reflected on the events that had taken placed. But I could not shake the feeling of being loved. The next day when Johnny was driving me and his girlfriend home from school, he began telling her what had happened to me. We all busted out laughing when he told her I thought I was going to die. Before he dropped me off, he told me that he was going to be playing in a concert at the church on Saturday. He asked if I would like to go. I told him I wasn't sure I was ready yet. He said, "Come on man there're going to be plenty of girls there." I said, "Ok. I'm in!" I went shopping on Friday to buy some dress clothes and shoes. I hadn't been to church in a few years and I knew I couldn't wear any high waters up in there. Johnny picked me up and we headed there. I was very nervous. I had no idea what to expect. When I walked in I was shocked. There were young people everywhere, and a lot of cute girls. The concert began and he was up on stage. It was the first time I saw him play. He was amazing. On one song he had a solo and killed it! He was incredible! I was really having a good time, when all of a sudden my legs begin to vibrate. I started feeling that overwhelming presence of love again. I don't know why, but I wrapped my arms around myself and began to rock back and forth. I felt so safe. This time I knew what was going on. I knew this was the Holy Spirit introducing himself to me again. I remember saying, "God I want to be used." At this time a lady got up and started to sing this song. I didn't know what the song was then, but I know now. It's called, "Can You Reach My Friend," by Helen Bailer. As she was singing, I looked up and saw angels flying in a circular motion above this lady. I couldn't believe what I was seeing. Was this real? Was I the only one seeing this? Am I crazy? These are the questions I began to ask myself. I closed my eyes to rub them. I was hoping that everything would be normal when I opened them. But when I opened my eyes the angels were still there. They never left. I began to cry uncontrollably. I was broken. My heart was being cleaned. My mind was being renewed. When the lady stopped singing the song, they gave an altar call. As I started to walk to the altar the angels began to fly towards the ceiling and then they were gone. I publicly confessed Jesus as my Lord. I was so excited! For the first time in my life I thought like a winner! I looked like a winner! I felt like a winner! I talked like a winner! I walked like a winner! I was a winner!

•Tips for the Winner

There may be things that happen to you in life that you can't explain. Never waste time and energy trying to figure out the unexplainable! That's what faith is for! Just believe it, receive it and thank God for it.

Chapter 7

And the Journey Begins

"Starting today, let yesterday's pain become tomorrow's pleasure!"

~Anthony M. Fourshee

The next several months where transforming. My heart had completely changed. I no longer desired man's approval. I just wanted to know Jesus. I could not understand His love for me. I mean, why was I so important? Why me? What did I do? Or maybe it was something I was going to do.

I was starting my senior year and was hit with the pressure of what I was going to do with my life. Johnny had graduated and was starting school to be an auto mechanic. But I really had no idea what I really wanted to do with my life. To be honest, all I really wanted to do was go to church.

Because I had always had cooking classes, people assumed I wanted to be a chef. I never really thought about being a chef. The truth was, I cooked because I liked to eat, not because I liked to cook. But people in school assumed that I had this great, big passion for the culinary arts because I was good at it. As soon as school started, everyone noticed the change in me. And how could they not? The Lord had lit me on fire! I could not contain what He had done to me. I could not stop talking about his love and about the mask I was wearing. I began the share it with everyone. However, I never told anyone about seeing angels. I didn't want people to think I was crazy. I also felt that God allowed me to see them personally for a reason, and that He would reveal it in time.

    I recognized a couple of guys from the church at lunch period. These guys normally sat by themselves. They didn't have many friends outside of the church, so I went and sat with them. After a few days, many of my friends gave their lives to the Lord and they started to sit with us. In less than a month we had about 50 kids having Bible study at lunch. It was incredible how God was increasing, yet, I was still dealing with the issue of my future. My parents were constantly asking me about my future all the time, which I couldn't understand! I mean, it's not like I was a slacker or something.

When I was 15, my brother got me a full-time, summer job at a printing company, sweeping the floors, gathering cardboard, cleaning up, etc. The owners were so impressed with me, they kept me on part time after school. I had already been working there for many years, so I had a good work ethic. I guess my parents wanted more for me. They thought I was getting out of hand with this church stuff and needed to focus a little more on my future. But I didn't know what to say. I wasn't sure of what I wanted to do. I was just discovering who I was. I mean, I had worn this mask for all of these years. The things I used to do, I didn't want to do anymore. The places I used to go, I didn't want to go anymore. So, I pondered, "What am I going to do?"

I happened to be in the guidance office one day when there was a hand full of students in there. The students were all talking to the counselors about the colleges that they were applying to. One student was applying to Princeton, one to Syracuse, another to Howard and another to Temple. When one of the counselors asked me, I had no idea what to say. I didn't want to look like an irresponsible slacker so I blurted out, "I'm going to Johnson and Wales to become a pastry chef. I want to work on a cruise ship." I thought to myself, "Now where did that come from? I know I didn't just sit up here and lie like a rug to these people." They all were so impressed, because I had an original goal. I had mentioned something different and this intrigued them. They were more interested in my career path than the others. Suddenly, one of the counselors mentioned that she had just gotten a memo about a $24,000 scholarship for high school seniors for food service programs, and that I should apply. I thought, "Now what did my big mouth get me into!" In 5 minutes, I had put together something my brain couldn't do in months.

    A couple of days went by and the news had spread like a wild fire throughout the faculty. Every class I had, my teacher would come and say they heard I was applying for the Johnson and Wales scholarship and wished me good luck. I was starting to feel a sense of pride. Maybe this was what I was supposed to do. After all, I was pretty good at it. So I began to embrace it. I had to write an essay on what makes me unique. I wrote about the whole high school mask experience and how God had changed my heart. There were 5,000 applicants. A month later, I got a letter in the mail stating that there had been 9 finalist selected for the first round: 3 from North Jersey, 3 from Central Jersey and 3 from South Jersey. "Congratulations! You are one of the South Jersey finalists." I couldn't believe it! I thought back to how I almost failed the 3rd grade, how the seeds of faith watered with a little love and confidence were yielding fruit! I was a winner! I had purpose!

And I was destined to do great things! I believed this with all my heart. My faith had risen. I knew that Jesus was using me to draw men unto Him. I knew that this was what Johnny and his mom meant when they said that the Holy Spirt wants to use me. Revival was spreading throughout the school. It was actually cool to be a Christian.

On the way to the first interview for the scholarship, I had to take a dreaded 45-min drive with my dad--not that I hated being with my dad, just the exact opposite. You see, my dad rarely talked to me. He never spent time with me. We were like complete strangers. Every time I would go somewhere with him there would be no conversation: no, "How are you doing son?" or, "What's new in your life?"--nothing-- just him listening to his oldies. All I ever wanted was for my dad to notice me. I had been filled with so many disappointments and heartbreaks about that, but I had given that over to the Lord. I was concerned that the ride would have an emotional effect on me. I wanted to be on my "A" game. I prayed the whole drive. I felt so much peace in that car. I believe my dad felt it to. There was something unusual about him. They called me in for the interview, and as I was walking down the hall, my dad called my name. I stop and turned around, and he yells, "Good luck son!" The biggest smile gripped my face. I knew that it took my dad the whole car ride to get that out of his mouth.

All I recalled about the interview was introducing myself to the judges, then saying" Have a good night." I literally could not remember anything that happened. It was almost as if I blacked out. On the ride home, I was down on myself. I thought I had blown it for sure. But a week later, I got another letter in the mail. The letter stated that I was 1 of 3 finalists for the scholarship. The letter went on to say how impressive my interview was and that I should be very proud of myself. I didn't understand! "What did God do to those people?" I thought, "This must be that favor thing!" I began to thank and praise God. I nailed the next interview, as well and won the scholarship.

At the awards banquet I had to give a little speech. And I remember telling them that nothing is impossible to those that believe, and that we can accomplish great things when we put our minds to it. But we can accomplish even *greater* things if we unlock the power of God inside us.

•Tips for the Winner•

Be an original, not a counterfeit, because you were made an original! There is nobody else in the world that can bring what you bring to the table. You have world changing potential inside of you! So use it!

Chapter 8

Vocalizing Your Victory

"You Gotta Start Somewhere! Everything in life has a birth. Life has a birth, dreams have a birth, and ideas have a birth."

~Anthony M. Fourshee

I must admit, winning that scholarship was pretty rewarding. And to think it all started with the power of my words. Believe it or not, words have world- changing power. They have the power to give life and take it away. I call it, vocalizing your victory! When I told those counselors, "I'm going to Johnson and Wales to become a pastry chef," I had no idea any of these things would be set in motion. When I blurted it out, it was a proclamation or an announcement to the atmosphere to get ready, because Anthony is going to do this. Now things could have gone completely different if I would have said it differently when I proclaimed what I was going to do. I didn't realize it at the time, but I proclaimed it boldly and with confidence. Now, if I would have sad, "Well, I'll thinking about possibly going to Johnson and Wales to hopefully become a pastry chef," my proclamation to the atmosphere would say, "Anthony's got something on his mind again; let's wait and see if he follows through with it this time!" You have the power to change your world with your voice. You have the power to be victorious in any situation you face. But it all starts with what's coming out of your mouth. You gotta start somewhere!

Everything in this world has a birth. Life has a birth: dreams have a birth, and ideas have a birth. But before all of these things come to pass they must have a verbal proclamation. They must have a verbal announcement.

It's amazing how God allows us the awesome honor to partner with Him in proclaiming our destiny. Notice I said partner? Yes, partner, meaning we have an authoritative decision to make with God that He wants and expects us to make. It's part of your maturing in Him.

A couple of weeks after the banquet, my mom and dad drove me up to Johnson and Wales in Providence, Rhode Island, for the scholarship recipient orientation. It was one of the worst road trips ever. First of all, it was pouring down raining. I mean it was coming down so bad that we had to stop several times because my dad could not see. Second of all, we had a blowout. Now I know you're thinking, "What's the big deal? Just call road-side assistance. Well that would be great if it wasn't 1991. Everyone didn't have cell phones yet. And my dad was probably the only dad in America who could not change a tire. He had to walk in the pouring rain to get help. We arrived at the orientation an hour late. We weren't the only ones. Apparently the storm delayed all of the festivities on campus. Each state had its own scholarship winner, which made this orientation a really a big deal, especially for the city of Providence. But the parade had been rained on and there wasn't much anyone could do about it.

Most of the entertainment had been moved indoors, like the ice-carving demonstration. This completely moves me. I mean, there is nothing more electrifying than watching someone transform a block of ice into a swan with a chainsaw. But for some reason, I could not enjoy it. I had this disturbing feeling in my gut. I walked over to this remarkably captivating cake display, filled with all kinds of delectably-designed cakes. I was completely wowed. I had never seen anything like it. I tried asking the head chef about the display, but he just ignored me. This was becoming a pattern. Everyone seemed to be ignoring us and giving us the cold shoulder. This was leaving a bitter taste in my mouth. After my parents and I watched everyone else mingle, we were called to meet with the financial dean about the funding. When we got in her office she explained that the scholarship was dispersed in four increments of $6,000.00 a year. But the school was $24,000.00 a year. She went on to say that I could not work, bring a car there or live outside of the dorms for the first two years. And the dorm rooms where 8- person dorm rooms. I could not believe it! I was so disappointed. This was not what I was interested in. To think that I would be putting an $18,000.00-a-year burden on my parents, I wouldn't have any money, no car and be stuck sleeping in a room with 8 guys, like I'm in the Army or something! I'll pass! But as the saying goes, "When one door closes, God opens another!"

The next day when we got back home, there was a letter addressed to me from Burlington County College. Apparently they were launching a new pastry chef program, and they wanted me to be a part of the launch. The new director of the program had seen me on television and thought that I would be a great start to the program. (My high school, audio/visual team recorded several baking programs of me that year and would run them constantly on our town's local, TV channel.

The channel only came on in the middle of the night. I thought that nobody watched that channel. But I guess I was wrong.)

They offered me a full scholarship with no out-of-pocket expenses. Just like I said before, sometimes in life, what you expect to be your break through won't be, but what you least expect will be."

•Tips for the Winner•

Did you know that you have the power to change any situation? Life and death is in the power of your tongue. So you can literally speak life over any situation! You can birth greatness by declaring greatness from your lips! So no matter how bad the situation may seem, you have the power to change it by your verbal declaration. You are what you speak!

Chapter 9

Go with Your Gut!

I really was excited to be the first to start the new program. I felt like a trailblazer, a trend setter. And to think, they wanted me to be the first to launch this program. I felt like a super star. But stars have been known to fall from grace. Well, I fell pretty hard after getting hit with some pretty hurtful words from my aunt. A couple of days after the trip, my mom was telling my aunt about what happened at Johnson and Wale. She went on to tell her about the extra money it was going to cost to send me there. She also told her about the full scholarship I got to Burlington County College, and how I was so excited about being chosen to launch that program. My aunt looked over at me and said, "You need to go to that big school in Rhode Island. Burlington County College ain't shxx. That new program ain't going to be shxx, and you ain't going to be shxx if you go there."

Talk about straight to the point! I felt like her words had jumped out of her mouth, onto my chest and commandeered any form of excitement that was hovering around my heart. The spirit of defeat would once again return to reclaim my thought process. It had escaped its prison where faith, trust and dependency on God had kept the spirit bound up. But the detestable suffocating presence had been loosed by a verbal destructive assignment. Those words my aunt spoke over me were designed to kill my dream and destroy my future. Have you ever heard of the saying, "Sticks and stones may break my bones but words will never hurt me?" Well, whoever came up with that was not being honest. I know firsthand because I was in pain.

I went over Johnny's house to talk to him about the recent events. I hadn't talked to him since the trip, and he had no idea what was going on with me. But one thing was for certain, Johnny was not happy about me going to Rhode Island: Not that he wasn't happy for me. He was one of my biggest cheer leaders. He thought he would be losing a great friend. And eventually we would just grow apart. He really wasn't ready for that right now. John knew he needed me. He needed my strength. He needed my courage. He needed me to help him get through one of the scariest times of his life--fatherhood. You see, John had gotten his longtime girlfriend Quaitra pregnant his senior year in high school. In fact, she was actually pregnant when we first started hanging out. John's parents divorced when he was younger. He never really shared the details of him and his father's relationship, except that it was full of empty promises. I recall sermons from John's mom about how God had delivered her out of the abuse she suffered from him. In my mind I had this picture of this evil man. But John never spoke against him--at least not to me, other than him saying he wasn't going to be like him. John vowed that no matter what happened, he was going to be a vital part of his son's life. He was determined not to be another statistic of a young black teen running away from his responsibility. He felt as if a God had entrusted him with the honor of rectifying the generational implications of fathers abandoning their children. However, he was terrified. He was taunted by fears of failing as a father. He knew what it felt like not being able to count on your father, and he didn't want that for his kid.

Quaitra had their son the summer after John graduated. This was a huge transition for both of them. You see, now the decision that they made affected not only their own life, but their baby's life. John asked me for a lot of advice, but who was I to give advice, especially on relationships? I was a fake player! I had a lot of girls around me and went on many dates, but I never found anyone I could be real with. I never found anyone who loved me without the mask. John loved Quaitra, and she loved her some Johnny! They were the poster children of high school sweet hearts. Their love was strong enough to stand the test of time.

When I got over Johnny's, he was home by himself, just playing around on his bass. Now John was a brilliant bass player. He had this zone thing he would go into when he'd play. You know how Michael Jordan would stick out his tongue when he was in a zone? Well, Johnny would close his eyes and bite down on his bottom lip with his front teeth. When he went to that place he was on fire. When I walked in, he was at that place. He was in such a zone, he didn't hear me come in. I sat there for about 5 minutes just listening to him play. I thought to myself, "How did he get to be so good! He must have had lessons in the womb!" I busted out laughing with the thought of his grown face on a newborn's body holding a bass.

This was funny to me, but I knew it wasn't true. John had only been playing for about 8 months when I first saw him play at that church. God had supernaturally taught him to play. He never had a lesson before. He just picked up the bass and started playing it. However, he didn't become great at it until he started having what I call zone outs. John would often tell me that he didn't remember what he played when that happened. He said it was as if a presence took over his body and he zoned out. When John first told me that, I didn't understand. But I understand now. The presence that John was referring to is the Holy Spirit. And when He, the Holy Spirit, came upon John in those zones out times, He took control. This allowed Jonny to worship his Heavenly Father in the spirit. That's why he didn't recollect what he played or remember what happened, because his natural mind was not in a state of awareness. Now I understand what happened to me at that dance my freshman year. The Holy Spirit was the one who anointed my body to dance like that. That was not in my natural abilities. That was completely super natural.

After my outburst of self-amusement, Johnny realized I was there. He was so excited to see me. John and his family had a way of making any and every one feel special. They always showed so much excitement in greeting you. Trust me; it was something you could never get used to. I told him all about the trip and what went down. I also told him about the letter, the new program and what my aunt said. I started getting a little upset. Immediately John said, "You never make any decision when you're upset!" I began to smile because I knew what was coming next. John began chanting in the Cookie Monster's voice, "cookies, cookies, cookies, cookies!"

You see, he had this thing where he thought that Chips Ahoy chocolate chip cookies could solve any of the world's problems. He would break them up in a bowl and eat them like cereal. He grabbed two bowls, some milk and cookies and we went to town. After a couple of minutes the smacking began to slow down. I knew it was time for his big finish. And that was to drink the now chocolate milk from the bowl. And he did just that. He gently sat his bowl on the counter, looked over at me with this serious looking face, and said, "Don't be upset with your aunt. She thinks she's helping you. In her mind she sees an opportunity for you to be the first in your family to go to a prestigious university like that. And she just doesn't want you to give that up. However, you gotta do what's going to make you happy. They are your choices to make--not your parents', aunt's or anyone else's. You make your own choice, and you live with that choice. But before you choose, listen to this tape." He hands me this tape called, "Speak to My Heart Lord," by Donnie McClurkin. For the next couple of weeks I could not put anything else in my tape player. God was speaking to my heart, and I knew for certain that I wasn't going to Johnson and Wales. I really didn't want to take the other scholarship either. I wanted to do something for God. But I thought it was a little late in the game for that. So I took the Burlington County College scholarship and headed there in the fall.

•Tips for the Winner•

Never be afraid of making a bad decision. And don't live in regret because you feel like you've made one. A bad decision may get you a little off track, but you will get to your appointed destination!

Chapter 10

There Is a War!

"Success is not defined by your current situation. Success is defined by your willingness to get out of your current situation."

~Anthony M. Fourshee

Do you realize that there is a war going on right now! Do you realize that battle lines are being drawn? Strategies are being cultivated. Spies are being implanted. Relationships are being severed. Love ones are becoming expendable. Fear is plaguing the land. Famine and poverty control the masses. People around you are drowning in their sluggish pits of stagnancy, routinely rotting away from the stench of mediocrity. You are on the front lines. And you, my friend, have been given a choice: a choice to sit and drown like everyone else around you, or to stand up, fight and take back what God has already given you. God has not given you a spirit of fear. He has given you love, power, and a sound mind. You must unlock the power inside you. You must draw from His love and visualize yourself winning *before* you win! You must understand: you cannot give up, you can't quit! Where you are today, is not where you'll be tomorrow! Right now you may be struggling financially, you may be dealing with some sort of loss, or you may have gotten a bad medical report. Whatever the situation is, you must declare that you are going to win! You must speak to the situation and put it in its place; because if you don't, it will speak to you and silence your voice. I know for a fact, that God has birthed a dream inside of you. And you have let life tell you that dreams don't come true. Well, I'm here to tell you to close your eyes, because your about to dream again! You may or may not feel it, but something is beginning to come alive on the inside of you. You have been elected for success! So go get it! There are gifts on the inside of you that the world is waiting with great anticipation to see. Don't let doubt steal your blessing!

Has God ever given you a great idea for something? I mean an idea that can change your life, but soon after this great breakthrough of wisdom, doubt comes in; and before you know it, that idea you had is a distant memory? Doubt comes in very quickly and quietly. It starts out small, and before you know it, your eyes are focused on what you *can't* do rather than what you *can* do. You see, that idea was your blessing, but instead of pursuing it, you let it go. Don't let doubt steal your blessing! If God gives you an idea, He's going to provide the means for it to come alive. God is the source, and He knows how to complete a task! What I mean by God being your source is, He's the one who supplies your needs-- not your job, your clients or customers. They are just ways that God chooses to bring provision to you. But if you look to Him for provision, by acknowledging Him as your source, He promises to provide your every need! If you trust in Jesus, He will give you the ability to get the job done. Remember, it's not your strength, but His strength. It's not your power, but the power of the Holy Spirit working in you and for you. So the next idea you get, remember: it's your blessing, so seek the face of Jesus and act on it!

Success is not defined by your current situation. Success is defined by your willingness to get out of your current situation. Have you ever struggled with something and just quit because it got too hard? Well, why did it get too hard? maybe because you didn't see the reward worth more than the sacrifice. You see, we quit too soon because many times we perceive that the benefits don't out weight the sacrifice. God requires us to live a life of sacrifice first. What he is teaching us is to find the reward actually in the sacrifice, not receiving a reward just because you made it through the sacrifice.

Everyone struggles in life. We all have battles. You know how the saying goes: "You win some, you lose some" But a winner doesn't think like that. A winner's perspective says "You win some, you learn some."

Many of us want change in our lives, but very few of us take the steps to change. Change is a choice. God will give you all the tools that you need to change, however tools are of no use if you don't use them. If you are talking about changing, you are already being surpassed by someone who is changing. However, you cannot change on your own. You must allow the Holy Spirit to change you. You see, if we try to change on our own, eventually we will get tired and quit. But if you let God come in and allow the Holy Spirit to overtake you, it becomes His strength, not yours. He is all you need to complete any task. No matter what your situation may be, God loves you and He will transform you if you let Him. And transformation is exactly what took place in me.

Chapter 11

Hitting the Road

"A star can light up the sky, but multiple stars light up the universe."

~Anthony M. Fourshee

A couple of years after high school, my life took another exciting turn. Johnny was playing the bass for a well-known professional gospel choir. They were recording their second album which was going to be a live recording. For about 3 months they had constant rehearsals. This all was extremely exhilarating to me. I got a chance to hang out with the band and see firsthand how the music creativity unfolded. I would be the first one there to help carry in equipment and the last one to leave to carry it back out. I wasn't getting paid like the musicians, but I was having a blast just hanging around those guys. I would bring my video camera and record the practice sessions for Johnny to go over later. I also would catch a lot of crazy bloopers and practical jokes from the guys just clowning around. One day the director of the choir said that he needed to talk to me. I thought to myself, "Man, he's going to tell me that I'm not allowed to hang out with the band anymore."

You see, they were all paid professionals and I was just a friend of one of those paid professionals. The director called me over and pulled me aside and said, "I've notice how attached you've gotten to the band. It's seems as if they really love having you around. You may not realize it, but you are really gifted with that video camera! I was wondering if you would consider being the choir's personal videographer. You can come on the road with us and videotape all of our concerts. We can't pay you, however you can set up a table before and after each concert and sell the videos. The money you make from the sales of the videos would be all yours and should cover any expenses you may have. All I ask is that you hook me up with a free video every now and then." Talk about jaw dropping! I was in complete shock! What an opportunity this was. Now this is a perfect example of why everything you do in life you do it as you are doing it for the Lord. You give your best in everything that you do, no matter what the circumstances are, no matter what the reward will be! You see,

I took joy in carrying in the equipment. I was never asked to do it. I saw a need and I did whatever I could do to help fill that need. I came early and stayed late, not to be seen or to get anything in return; I just wanted to be a blessing to those guys. And because of the pure motives that I had in my heart, God placed on the director's heart to create a position for me. How I gave of my time and energy in private, God rewarded me with a videographer position in public. A lot of times in our lives God is trying to promote us to a new level in life. He is trying to create new doors and opportunities to be opened to us. But, unfortunately, we are too busy sabotaging what He's trying to do with our selfishness and complaining. A winner thinks about the team first. Self-promotion is not in their DNA, because a true winner is confident in their abilities. A winner recognizes that connecting their gifting to someone else's gifting adds to the team. However, highlighting your own gifting only subtracts from the team and puts the spotlight and focus on you, which creates division. Look at it like this: a star can light up the sky, but multiple stars light up the universe.

Being on the road was exciting for the first couple years. Traveling to places like LA, San Francisco, Atlanta, Washington DC and New York was spectacular. However, after a while, I started to feel like we were all just entertainers.

I felt like we were no different from rappers or rock stars. Everything was about the performance and how the show went. I was the one filming night after night after night. I began to notice that everything was the same. I started to realize that everything we were doing was in our own natural abilities. It was almost as if we had to show God how to give a great performance. And that's exactly what it was-- a performance. I started to feel so distant and separated from God. I began to recognize everything as learned behavior-- everything from the way people preached to the way they praised God. To me it was all a routine. I remember crying out to God one day. I told Him that I wanted to settle down and get married.

    I had heard a preacher on TV talk about how he had written a letter to God describing what he wanted in a wife. Turned out that God had given him everything he put in the letter. So I decided to give it a shot. I figured I'd do exactly what the preacher did, but I would be a little more specific. I didn't want to take any chances on God saying "gotcha" because I wasn't specific. I chuckled at the thought of me and this beautiful woman running up towards each other on the beach. And just as I'm captivated by her beauty, she smiles and has only one rotten tooth in her mouth! Then I imagine God saying, "You didn't say she needed to have teeth!" I was not taking any chances. I was super specific in that letter. I put it in my Bible and went back to my life with the choir. About six months later, I got a call from a high school friend. I hadn't heard from her in a couple of years, so we were catching up on old times. She told me she had a friend who was on spring break and was staying over with her. I began to tell her all about the choir and how I've been traveling around the country. I could tell she really wasn't interested. She said that she really didn't know much about gospel music, but her friend really knew a lot about it. So she put her friend Tammy on the phone. As soon as she said hello, my knees began to buckle. I immediately had to sit down. Her voice was so soothing, comforting and gentle. Her laugh warmed my body like a cup of hot chocolate during a snow storm. I was captivated! I literally hung on every word she said. As each hour passed, her words began to surgically remove my heart through the phone lines. It was as if she was in my mind, in my thoughts. We talked for 4 hours straight. My high school friend never got the phone back. I could not wait until the next day to talk to Tammy again. I called her back the next day and we talked like 6 hours straight. I fell completely in love with this woman, and I had no idea what she looked like. The thing is, she knew what I looked like, because her friend had a lot of pictures of me. But I was completely in the dark. I had to trust God! I had to believe that He would not fail me. They invited me over and I couldn't get there fast enough! As I knocked on the door, Tammy opened it. Now, imagine opening a box of Cracker Jack's, expecting to find a sticker for a prize. But instead of finding a sticker in the box, you find a rare, one- in-a-million priceless, 20-carat blue diamond. That's how I felt when I laid my eyes on Tammy. She was simply breath taking! Her eyes were so enchanting. Her smile was mesmerizing! I was captivated by her perfectly formed white teeth. Thank God I was specific!! I thought to myself, "She is out of my league! This girl is too beautiful for me!" But God already had it worked out.

Chapter 12

This Girl Gets Me!

"I realize that before the foundation of the world was created, God had set aside this masterfully design plan to infuse our hearts together."

~Anthony M. Fourshee

It was an incredible experience meeting Tammy face to face. I truly had a wonderful time with her. This girl got me! I mean she really got me! Tammy looked at me in a way that no other woman had ever looked at me before. As her eyes wondrously gazed into mine, I believe I caught a glimpse of something magical through the windows of her soul. It reminded me of the childhood joys of looking into a department store window at Christmas time. But it was more than that! It was like somehow her eyes released electrical pulses that stimulated every fiber of my being! Gently and intentionally she shifted her pretty browns to fixate on my lips. As if she somehow needed my words for strength. As if every syllable that catapulted out of my mouth directed her heartbeat. Words cannot describe the overwhelming exuberance that filled the room that day! I realized that before the foundation of the world was created, God had set aside this masterfully designed plan to fuse our hearts together. I didn't know it at the time, but months later, Tammy would tell me about how God had shown her in a dream, me and her standing over the top of my oldest son's crib. She went on to say that she didn't know who I was at the time. But when she saw my picture at her friend's house, the memory of the dream came back to her. She also said that night when we met, she felt this powerful magnetic pull drawing her to me. And when I left, she felt like she was supposed to leave with me. There is no way Tammy nor I can argue the fact that God supernaturally fused us together. I had never been in love before, but I felt like our relationship was kind of unique! I mean, the way I always thought dating went was, you take a girl out to get to know her. The more you get to know her the more you will like her. And then maybe, if you're lucky, she could be the one. Well it didn't happen like that with me. You see, I was sold before I had even seen what she looked like! Do you remember that famous scene from the movie Jerry Maguire? When Renee Zellweger's character said, "You had me at hello?" Well that's exactly how I felt. Tammy had me when she said hello on that phone call! And there was nothing I could do about it! I don't think I had ever met a women like Tammy before. She was really smart and intelligent. She was quiet, yet strong and full of courage. Her spirit was overflowing with generosity, and her heart's number 1 residence was compassion. She is the oldest of three kids. Her brother Frank is a couple of years younger than she is, and her little sister Kara is 7 years younger. Her father is a minister, and her mother was the director of the youth education department at their church. When Tammy was growing up as a kid, church was literally an everyday- of-the-week experience. Tammy and I were inseparable. Johnny and the band absolutely loved her. I loved it when she would come to the concerts and see me in action filming. I had to let everyone know that she was the future Mrs. Fourshee. That didn't go over too well with everyone, especially my stalker! Well maybe the word "stalker" might be a little harsh. But the woman thought that she was my fiancée!

There was this woman who would constantly tell me that God told her that I was her husband. It seemed as if every service this woman would come up to me with this crazy nonsense. At first it was a little funny. Johnny and the guys would laugh and tease me about her. The woman was really close with John's family and at one point used to be a friend of mine. But that had all changed and the situation was starting to get out of hand. Constantly, everywhere I went, she would show up with her craziness. The stress of all of this was taking a serious toll on me. I was getting very angry and upset with the direction of her motives. One particular service, Tammy was with me, and this woman stood up in front of the whole church and said all of this crazy stuff about me leaving Tammy to be with her. I couldn't take it anymore. I could not take a chance on my future being ruined by this deranged starker. So I quit! I quit the choir, I quit going to church. I completely withdrew from everyone around me except Tammy. We became best friends. I gave up everything and everyone to be with her and she did the same for me.

Four hundred and eleven days after that face to face connection, Tammy did me the honor of becoming my bride. It only took one phone call to change my life! Imagine what one can do for you!

Chapter 13

The Power of Purpose

"Finding your purpose is not an event!"

~Anthony M. Fourshee

    The word "purpose" seems to be one of the most commonly used words in our current day. Everyone seems to be talking about finding your purpose, as if it were some deep, hidden treasure that's lost! Finding your purpose is not an event! Finding your purpose in its simplest form is finally understanding the reason why God created you and doing exactly what He created you to do with determination, passion and devotion.

    There is nothing more powerful in life than understanding your purpose or purposes. I truly believe that each and every one of us has multiple purposes in life. But we normally only discover one, maybe two of them. I think this is because we seldom take inventory of the process of our lives. Everything in life has a purpose. Everything in life--good or bad-- has a reason behind it. Just because we may not understand the meaning right now, or just because we may be feeling pain right now, doesn't mean that God isn't going to turn the current situation around for our good. Sometimes it takes some difficulties in life for us to learn to put our focus and attention on what's really important.

Remember in the previous chapter when I was telling you about the difficulties I was having with dealing with that woman claiming to be my wife? Because of that situation, I valued the importance of Tammy. She became my number 1 priority, behind God. When we married, we became one. You see, I discovered early on, in that first phone call with Tammy, that she was my purpose. I knew that the God of the universe who showers us with sunlight by day and who polishes us with breathtaking, star- filled moon light at night created me to wake up every morning just to put a smile on his daughter's face. I realized that I could not add value to something that was already priceless. However, I could wake up every morning and polish the diamond that God had given me, so it would shine as bright as it could possibly shine, without smudges or stains, without spots or cracks. So let me ask you this! If you are married, are you polishing your spouse so they too can shine as bright as they possibly can? If not, then why not? Some of you are living with diamonds that haven't been chiseled out of the rock yet! Some of you set your diamonds aside and they have fallen in the mud and gotten all dirty and mucky. Listen, the value is still there! You just need to work on chiseling that rock out of the wall. You just need to sit down and take some time to clean the mud and dirt off of it! Listen, it may take time, but it's worth it! Don't give up! Don't quit! And don't pawn it away! It's way too valuable!!!

Now I am by no means telling you that this is easy. But I am telling you this: anything in life that God gave you is worth fighting for! Quitting cannot be an option! You must fight without ceasing! It's not going to be easy! It's going to take work! It's going to take sacrifice! It's going to take swallowing your pride, denying your feelings and suppressing that urge to proclaim how right you are. But it can be done. And you, my, friend, can do it! You have all of the makings of a winner! You've been created to produce an unthinkable amount of possibility. But possibility can only be possible with one requirement: a decision! Yes, a decision! You must make a decision to shine your spouse! You must be determined to see your marriage strong, alive, thriving and continuously flourishing daily, with an expectation of "Where I am today, I'm not going to be tomorrow!" You must expect better in order to be better! You must expect more to get more! This not only applies to marriage, this applies to life! You are only going to get out of life the amount that you are willing to invest in your life. So what's your investment? Stop coasting! Stop surviving, and start thriving! Take a chance and get yourself in the game! You can't win if you don't start!

People are afraid to fail, but if you don't step out, you're already failing, because you're staying in the same spot. So what's the difference? Get moving and put action behind your tongue! You can do it, because you are a winner, and a winner never stops fighting!

Chapter 14

Obstacles Will Come

"Obstacles in life are just opportunities to show the world what an overcomer looks like!"

~Anthony M. Fourshee

The road on your journey towards success will be filled with obstacles, challenges and trials. No one is immune from them. Obstacles in life are just opportunities to show the world what an overcomer looks like! Trials seem to function on a three-stage time table. Those three stages are past, present and future. And every human is in one of the three stages right now in their own life. Either you have experienced a trial in the PAST, you are currently enduring a trial in the PRESENT, or you will meet up with a trial in the FUTURE. It doesn't matter what your background is. It doesn't matter how much money you have or how successful you are. As long as you are breathing, you are in one of those three stages in life. But if you happen to be reading this and you're not breathing, I think that you have bigger fish to fry! Your focus should never be on the trial or obstacles. A winner never highlights a problem, he only highlights the solution. The spotlight should always be targeted on the solution.

This is a lesson I learned the hard way. It was during one of the most difficult times in my life. In 2002, I had a tragic accident that rattled my world. I was working on the waterfront in Philadelphia as a ship builder. The company I worked for manufactured massive container ships. We would built the ships in sections and put the pieces all together like a puzzle. One day as a handful of my co-workers were preparing to weld a section together, one of the 5-ton chains that we had holding up the wall snapped like a rubber band, sending the chain soaring up like a missile. I just happened to be leaning down to inspect the measurements at the time the chain snapped. In a split second, I put my arm up to block the chain from hitting me in the head. Now, if you recall earlier, I mentioned how God had stopped time during my high school dance and how I could feel the emotions of the people at the dance. Well, this was a similar situation. After the chain snapped, I was squatting down in front of it, when all of a sudden time literally stopped. I was able to stand up and put my arm in front of my face. Then time resumed. The chain should have hit me in my face, killing me instantly. But instead, it hit me in my arm sending a jolt of pain down my arm like lightning! Miraculously, the missile-soaring chain didn't break my arm; however my arm swelled up like a balloon. I was diagnosed with a condition known as RSD (reflex sympathetic dystrophy.) It's also known as chronic pain syndrome.

The pain was unbearable! Imagine feeling like your blood is boiling all of the time. Imagine not being able to move your arm or fingers. The gentlest touch anywhere on my arm would create a lightning storm of pain! With each jolt it felt like someone taking a railroad spike and driving it into my elbow! And to add insult to injury, the insurance company cut my workman's compensation benefits. It felt like my world had collapsed and I was trapped under the rubble. We were forced to go on public assistance. My wife was a stay-at-home mother. She was home taking care of our two sons, Anthony and Alex. Anthony was around 3 years old at the time and Alex was 1. Our income was completely gone, and along with it went my dignity. We had to move in with my parents just to survive. I began to spiral into depression. You see, all I was doing was focusing on the problem, not the solution.

Every time I went to the doctor I had the expectation of a negative report. My mind was so twisted up at the time because it was problem driven. If my doctor didn't tell me things were getting worse, I would get very upset. I enjoyed sympathy. I felt sorry for myself and expected others to join in my pity party. I was getting injections in my spine and elbow to ease the pain. I was on all kinds of pain killers. My doctor told me that the disease had spread throughout my body. He said that I would be disabled for the rest of my life. I was told to expect the worst, because I would be totally debilitated with no hope of recovery. This played right into my "stinking thinking."

After hearing the doctor say that I wasn't getting any better, Tammy decided to go to school for medical coding. She realized that our roles had to be reversed, knowing that I wouldn't be able to work anymore. She stepped up to the plate to embark upon the role as the "breadwinner" for the family. She was completely focused on saving our family. Unlike me, her mind was targeted on the solution. She had a plan--the winning formula to change the recipe of disaster I had been using. Her plan was to be the best student she could possibly be, graduate with honors and secure a job to support our family. She was determined to change our situation! She was determined not to let our current situation define who we were! Determination is the driving force to success! It's what wakes you up in the morning. Determination is what catches the tears at night and transforms them to fuel in the morning. After several years of dedication and hard work, Tammy graduated valedictorian of her class and landed a great job. Everyone was so proud of her. In my heart was an explosion of admiration. I mean, think about it. This woman already had the most overworked and underpaid position in the world as a stay-at-home mother. And now to add nurse, chef, maid and full-time student to the responsibility check list is completely overwhelming, even to the superman. But Tammy did it! And she did it with humility and delight!

My wife taught me a valuable lesson about being solution focused. She set a goal despite our circumstances. Not only did she achieve her goal in graduating, but she was valedictorian! A winner knows how to hurdle over obstacles because they're not focusing on the obstacles. The solution must always be your goal. So remember, the next time you are hit with a trial, don't let it move you. Focus all of your attention on solving it, because you're a winner! And winners make things happen!

Chapter 15

You Are Not Alone

Shortly after Tammy started her new job, everything seemed to be falling into place. My perspective began to change. We had income coming in. Not only from Tammy's job, but my lawyer had managed to get my workman's compensation started back up, along with 9 months of back money they owed me. Things had dramatically changed in our lives. We were happy again. However, I was still dealing with the chronic pain. In my mind I figured this was my new life. And honestly, I just had to except it.

After a couple of months on the job, Tammy began to develop some weird numbing feelings in her legs. She attributed it to her change in lifestyle. She figured it was from going from a stay-at-home mom, to a full-time student, and now to a full-time worker. She chalked it up to be added stress on her body. So she just shrugged it off and kept going. A couple of weeks later she noticed that the tingling was increasing, and she started seeing double. Now, this was a major cause for her concern meter to rise. While hanging out with her sister and her sister's friend, she asked her sister's friend about it. Her sister's friend was a massage therapist and knew a lot about the human anatomy. She immediately told Tammy that it sounded neurological and that Tammy should see a neurologist immediately. The next day Tammy was on the phone making an appointment.

    During that first visit with the neurologist Tammy was extremely nervous. The neurologist physically examined Tammy, then he sat us down to give us his diagnosis. He told us that the symptoms she was having could be linked to several different things. However, he believed that the symptoms could be related to MS (multiple sclerosis). He wasn't certain. He said it had to be confirmed with a MRI. I can vividly recall the expression on Tammy's face. It was completely blank! Like a deer caught in headlights. Tammy was paralyzed by fear! "How could this be? Is this a joke?" shouted from her blank face. Tammy had the MRI a couple of weeks later. And yes, MS was confirmed. Talk about a punch in the gut! This was life- altering news. I have always heard people say, "God wouldn't put more on you than you can bear." And I must admit, this was feeling a little unbearable. "Why are you punishing us!" shouted my wounded heart, as I piled yet another disappointing trial onto our list of hardships. I threw my bucket down our well of hope only to pull up dried dirt. My well was empty! My hope was gone! I felt abandoned, like a baby left on the doorstep of a foreclosed house. "Is this God's plan for our lives?" was the question I asked myself. Once again I sent out invitations to my spectacular pity party. I felt sorry for us. To be honest, it was really hard to find faith in all of this. How can any good come out of this? Looking back now I realize that those particular trails spring boarded us into our destiny. Tammy handled our situation completely different. She handled it with complete confidence and faith. From her perspective, she knew that she knew that God would get us through this. The doctor immediately put Tammy on medication. At the time, there was no oral medication for multiple sclerosis, so Tammy was taking injectable medication. She ended up having an allergic reaction to the medication. From this reaction she could no longer function the way she previously did. She could not get out of bed or move around at all. In a matter of one week, my wife went from superwoman to bedridden.

•Tips for the Winner•

Life may side track you and punch you in the gut. Even though it may hurt for a minute, the pain is short-lived. It only lasts for a moment! So get up and punch back! Winners may fall down, but they don't stay down.

Chapter 16

Tired of Being Sick and Tired

"When you find yourself in a pit, don't focus on the pit or focus on how you got in the pit. Shift all of your energy on the one who can get you out of the pit."

~Anthony M. Fourshee

  After Tammy's diagnosis, I felt like our world was spiraling out of control. I felt depressed, discussed, derailed and plenty of other" D" words. All of the medications I was on didn't exactly help either. You see, not only was the medication suppressing my physical pain, it was suppressing my emotional pain. I was being "zombie-ized." My thinking was like a living dead man. But instead of brains, my cravings were for people to feel sorry for us. Honestly, I needed people to feel sorry for us to survive. I was a poster child for wo- is-me syndrome. It was the only thing that kept me going at the time. I can recall one day being in the grocery store and this lady came up to me. She said to me, "God told me that He is going to heal you. And after He heals you, you are going to get a nice settlement." My immediate thoughts were, "this lady is wacko!" So I just smiled and said thank you. As I walked away I remember thinking to myself, "This lady has gotta be crazy! How am I going to get a settlement if I'm healed?" I was in a place of doubt and unbelief.

Tammy on the other hand was strong! She refused to give up or give in! She began to seek God for answers. Her faith became contagious! Her relentless pursuit of God changed the atmosphere in our home. The passion for Christ she had grew just as strong in me as it was in her. We needed to know who this Jesus dude really was!!

Our pursuit for Jesus was not on a religious level, it was on a personal level. I mean, both of us had already taken the class of Church 101. We knew the church lingo; we knew all of the things that were expected of a believer to do and how to act. However, I didn't really know Christ. I mean KNOW Him Know Him, like when I was first introduced to Him. For me, everything was on the surface. And quite frankly I wanted to go deeper. Both my wife and I were not satisfied with what we had. We wanted more! We wanted His presence! We wanted His favor! We wanted to see His face! No longer was I focused on the pit I was in. No longer was I reliving in my mind the events that led us up to our current situation. His face was all I needed.

My wife and I began watching Christian TV for answers. There were many shows we watched on a regular basis, but there was one in particular that stood out from the rest. It was called, "Its Supernatural" by Sid Roth. The show was about people who had incredible experiences and encounters with God. Sid Roth would interview them as they tried to explain the experiences they had. This show totally draws you in. Our faith began to skyrocket each and every time we watched.

One particular episode really grabbed me! It was an interview with Gary Oates. In this episode, Garry Oates talked about how the Lord supernaturally opened his eyes to see angels. He also talked about how he was experiencing supernatural miracles. This jumped out at me! Suddenly, my memory bank was jolted with a deposit from the past. I began to recall the night I went to Johnny's concert as a teen. I remembered the feelings of unexplained excitement as I witnessed angels flying above the songstress as she sang. I never understood it before. I never heard anyone else talk about seeing angels before. Now I knew for certain that I was not crazy. I knew that someone else had experienced a similar encounter. On the show, Garry Oates also talked about how he had written a book about his experiences. The book was called, *Open My Eyes Lord*.

I suddenly felt it was time for me to seek understanding of my own personal experience. And maybe this was the direction that God was leading both Tammy and me. So we ordered his book. I've never been much of a reader; in fact, I outright hated reading. For me reading was a chore, like taking out the trash, painting the house or raking leaves on a Saturday! I'm more of a visual learner. Anytime in the past that I had ever made an attempt to read a book always ended the same way--with me in a deep, coma-like sleep and a pulsating crick in my neck. But for some reason, I was completely overwhelmed with excitement! Deep down in my spirit I had a feeling that this book would be a game changer for both Tammy and me. I felt like there was a reason for us to read this book. And the reasons would be great, yet, beyond our comprehension.

Chapter 17

No Pain, No Gain

"Adversity is the fertilizer to life. Without it, there is no growth."

~Anthony M. Fourshee

I've heard many people in my life quote that old saying, "no pain, no gain." As much as I hate to admit it, it really is true! I think we all want to live our lives free from problems. But what if God in His grace-releasing wisdom allows us to encounter problems to take us to another level in our lives?

"Adversity is the fertilizer to life. Without it, there is no growth." Please go with me for a moment. What if every problem, every loss, every pain and turmoil was an opportunity for you to live in God's peace? Jesus said,

These things I have spoken to you, that in Me you may have peace. In the world you will have tribulation; but be of good cheer, I have overcome the world." (John 16:33 NKJV)

This is one of my favorite verses in the bible. I think it's one of my favorites because it really sums up life. Think about it! The first thing that jumps out at you is PEACE. Jesus told us about having tribulation in life so we wouldn't get stressed out or in fear. If Jesus spoke peace unto us, why is it that when we are faced with challenging times, peace seems to be the last thing on our minds. There must be a reason. He mentions this. He tells us that in this world we will have tribulation. To paraphrase it, He's saying, " Look, y'all about to go through some stuff! Some things aren't going to be fair. You are going to have some disappointments. You are going to have some heart breaks. Things aren't always going to go your way in life." You see, He was preparing us for the hardship! He was letting us know what was going down before it ever went down. He was giving us a blue print for success! A teacher always tells you what's going to be on the test before you ever take it. But if you never pay attention and listen you will never know what's on the test.

When I was in school, I hated to learn. I never paid attention in class. So whenever the teacher was teaching I would not listen. Whenever the teacher would say study this because it's going to be on the test, it would go in one ear and right out the other. So when test time came, of course I failed because I never listened to the teaching! I never listened to the warning that this is going to be on the test. Of course I never took responsibility for it. I would blame the teacher and say, "You never told us this was going to be on that test." Well, that's sort of the same thing we do with Jesus. He told us that we would have tribulations in life. Yet, we feel caught off guard when things happen in life. Even though we were told that stuff was going to happen. The next thing he says is,"But be of good cheer for I have overcome the world." In other words, get excited because I have fixed it for you to win! He has prepared it so every outcome in life would benefit us for good. He's telling us not to focus on the situation, which may seem bad at the time, but focus on the victory! You see, He knows that you are going to come out of it stronger. He knows that you're going to be wiser. He knows that by you going through this particular situation, you will be able to help someone else out in the future who may be going through the same thing. He has already giving us the answers to pass the test. However, we must listen, go back and study our notes before the test is even given.

•Tips for the winner•

God has set us up to win in life, not fail! If we feel like we are failing maybe it's because we are focusing on the wrong things. Shift gears by changing your focus to the positives of the situation rather the negatives of the situation.

Chapter 18

F•E•A•R

"When there is fear, faith cannot be found! When there is faith, fear melts away like a candy bar on a hot beach!"

~Anthony M. Fourshee

One of the main ingredients that keep people from having a winner mentality is fear. Fear will sabotage your destiny. Fear can crush your dreams, foil your future and outright dismantle friendships. Fear takes your hopes and sprinkles failure on the seeds before they can even take root. Fear will silence your voice and prevent you from speaking out. Fear will cause you to lie, cheat and even kill to protect itself.

For most of us, fear plays the leading role in this journey we call life. I know for me, fear played a massive role in the lives of both me and my family, especially after Tammy's diagnosis and my accident. But what fear doesn't want you to know is that faith has power over fear. Faith is fear's worst enemy. When there is fear, faith cannot be found! When there is faith, fear melts away like a candy bar on a hot beach!

I like to refer to FEAR as:

Frequently

Escaping

Abnormal

Reality

After Tammy and I read that book, our perspectives began to change. No longer did we settle for the fear factor. We began fighting fear with faith! We committed ourselves to truly believing the promises God said in the Bible. We were determined to believe that spiritually, physically and financially we were blessed and favored. I can recall the first time this was put into practice.

Gary Oates, the guy who wrote the book, *Open My Eyes Lord* was going to be at a conference in our state. The conference was being held at a church that was about 2 hours away from us. When we heard about him coming, we were super excited. At this particular time, we were really hungry for more. We no longer wanted to live a religious life. We wanted to live the life that Jesus had intended for all believers to live--a life full of abundance! Unfortunately at this time, we were not living an abundant lifestyle. To put it in simple terms, we were broke! We were barely making ends meet. We had an old Mercury Cougar that was on its last leg. The A/C was broken and the transmission was hanging on by a thread. Both Tammy and I felt like we were supposed to go see Gary Oates. We felt like this is what God wanted us to do. The conference was 3 days long, which meant that we would have to get a hotel room for 2 days and need money for gas and food. Also, we would most likely have to rent a car, because I didn't think "Betsy" (our cougar) would make it up there and back. It was looking like this trip was going to be out of our financial ability. However, we could not shake the feeling like we were supposed to go. So we did the opposite of what our naturally, fear-filled minds wanted us to do. We decided to pray and believe that God would meet our needs. I remember praying specifically, "God, we are going to this conference because we believe you want us to go. So we go in Jesus' name believing you to supply our needs."

    We had enough gas money to get up there and go to the first service, which stared at 8 am. As we walked into the service the atmosphere was incredible! Everyone was singing and dancing. A cloud of joy was hovering around that place. I had never been in a church before where people were so free to worship God like that. We were having a great time. As the first session began to end and break for lunch, Tammy and I were trying to decide what to do for lunch. We only had $20 to our name. And even that needed to last us the entire weekend. As we started walking out of the church, a lady came up to us. She said to us," I'm sorry to bother you, but as I was sitting in the service the Lord told me to give you all the money I have." She went on to say," I'm new to hearing from God. I feel deep in my heart that I'm supposed to give you this." She handed me a hundred dollars. Tammy and I were in shock! We couldn't believe it! God actually told someone to give us money, someone who we never saw or met before. This was incredible! We began to just thank and praise God. We had heard about supernatural provision in books before. However, it had never happened to us! It hadn't even happened to anyone else we've known before. This was incredible! The lady had a crazy look of confusion on her face. She didn't know what was going on with us. Like she said, she was new to hearing from God. And we were new to receiving from God. I began to explain to her how we came here in faith! I told her how this was the first time we made a conscious decision to step out and trust God. She began to get excited also because she knew that she had heard right from God. It took a few minutes for all of us to get our composure back. The lady said she had to go run a few errands before the start of the next service. So we parted ways.

Tammy and I were so excited we could hardly eat our lunch. The reality that God loved us so much, that He would make sure we had lunch on Him. After lunch we headed back for the next service. As we were getting ready to find our seats, the lady came back up to us and handed me a bank envelope with hundreds of dollars in it. I said, "What is this? You already gave us money!" She said to us, "You don't understand. God told me to give you guys ALL the money I had. So I went and emptied my bank account out." She went on to say, "It's not much, but it's all I have right now." Talk about jaw dropping! She said it was not that much, but to us it felt like a million dollars. It was enough to cover the rental, the hotel, gas and food. We even had enough to buy books and CDs at the gift table. This was really amazing!

After the second service this same lady—Mary--invited us to her house for dinner. I felt a little reluctant at first. I mean, all of this was new to us. Someone we didn't even know giving us all of this money, now, inviting us to dinner! We've never experienced hospitality like this before, and it was making me nervous. After talking with Tammy, we decided to go. Tammy felt like God was up to something. And she was curious to see what it was he was up to. As we headed out following her in our rental, the drive seemed to take forever. I mean, I just assumed that the lady lived around the corner or something. I didn't realize that she live 45 minutes away. We were seeing a side of Jersey that we never saw before. We drove through woods, farmland, up and down hills. I kept having these thoughts that she was taking us to the middle of nowhere to rob us and take her money back. I was so relieved when we pulled into a nice housing development.

    She had a beautiful house. Her lawn was freshly cut with straight diagonal lines. It reminded me of a professional baseball field. Her walkway was neatly edged, and all of her shrubs were trimmed evenly. I was really impressed! As we walked in I was pleasantly surprised to smell fried chicken. I began to smile. Tammy asked what was I smiling about, and, of course, I said nothing. But the truth is, I was thinking about the story of Hansel and Gretel. I thought that maybe the lady was trying to fatten us up so she could eat us. The thought of me getting in a pot made me laugh. Mary had called her daughter ahead of time and asked her to fry some chicken so it would be ready for us when we arrived. However, dinner was not quite ready yet. This gave us a chance to talk and get to know Marry a little better. She didn't really go into her personal life right away. She mainly talked to us about the new experiences she was having from God. She was telling us that she has been going to the church for about a year now. She didn't want to say how she was so far out of her comfort zone. She had never experienced church like she has been experiencing in the last year. She didn't understand what was going on, but she knew it was God. Her daughter finally came out of the kitchen. "Dinner is ready," she said in a soft, sad voice. Mary's daughter seemed so sad. She was only 19 years old, and it looked as if she was pregnant. I couldn't really tell because her stomach wasn't really big, but I assumed she was. She didn't really talk or eat much. She kind of just played with her food with her fork. I could really tell something was heavy on her mind. After dinner, I checked the time and realized it was getting late. We told Mary that we didn't want to be late for the last service. So we headed back to the church.

Before the service started, I had the overwhelming feeling to pray for Mary, her daughter and her grandbaby. The truth is I wasn't even sure if she was pregnant or not. I asked Mary if it would be alright for me to pray for her. She said sure. So Tammy, Mary and I held hands as I began to pray. I recall praying for her daughter's health. I felt like she needed both physical and emotional healing. I also began to pray for her unborn child. I felt like the baby's health was in question, so we prayed for a healthy baby and a healthy delivery. To be honest, I wasn't even sure if she was pregnant or not! The words just came out of my mouth. As I was praying for her unborn grandbaby, Mary started uncontrollably crying. I continued praying and she continued crying. Tammy began to comfort her. She hugged and rubbed her back. After a few minutes Mary began to calm down. Tammy asked her if everything was alright. Mary replied," These are tears of joy not sorrow. I'm sorry I didn't tell you this, but my daughter is HIV positive. She also is 6 months pregnant. I haven't told anyone this because I'm so embarrassed and ashamed. I've been asking God to not allow the baby to be born with HIV and for him to heal my daughter. I've been too afraid of judgement to ask for prayer. But you prayed for health and healing for my daughter and unborn grandbaby without me even saying anything, without even knowing that she was even pregnant. I know for a fact that was God. And I know now that they will be all right!"

After the service we exchanged numbers and said goodbye. Four months later Mary told us that her daughter had a litter girl who was born HIV free! Also, amazingly, her daughter's HIV was reversing itself! Her blood count levels were miraculously turning around! She was getting better and better day by day! As I reflect back on the encounter, it's amazing how God used Mary to meet our financial needs, and used us to meet Mary's emotional needs. I can't help but think, what if we continued to allow fear to govern our lives? What if we never stepped out in faith by going to the conference, believing that God would supply our financial needs? What if Mary never listened or did what God told her to do? God will meet you when you step out. Sometimes we try to figure everything out ahead of time. God wants you to walk through it step by step, holding his hand along the way. We are a living testament that He will supply your every need if you trust Him.

Tips for the Winner

God is in control! Go with his flow like a downstream river!

Chapter 19

Fatherhood

"The love of a father can never be measured or contained."

~Anthony M. Fourshee

As I stated previously, I believe everyone has several purposes. I told you Tammy was my first purpose. To be a husband, specifically her husband, is what God had predestined me to do. He also predestined me for fatherhood. I believe that there isn't anything more honorable than seeing the excitement of a child when their father comes home, or the enthusiasm of your child as they shout, "Daddy watch me!" as they attempt to fasciante you with some new adventurous skill they've learned. God has strategically given me the privilege to father two extremely talented individuals. I use the word individuals as an important barrier of separation, because each and every kid is unique! Each and every child has their own personality, purpose and giftings. As parents, it's Tammy and my job to recognize and identify these characteristics as early as possible and to place our children in an environment that will best nurture and grow whatever it is God has put on the inside of them.

Currently my oldest son, Anthony, is 18 years old, and my youngest son, Alex, is 15. Artistic creativeness has been floating around in Anthony's DNA since birth. Anthony's proficiency was overwhelmingly noticeable even in his ultrasound pictures. I mean, it was as if he had staged or planned his ultrasound pictures to be his announcement to the world, that he's coming to shake it up! I can remember Anthony as a toddler skillfully drawing with intent. The funny thing is, I don't think I can even remember him ever scribbling. His skill level always seemed to be a step above the rest. Anthony has always been incredibly smart and super intelligent. To be honest with you, this really intimidated me. It intimidated me because I felt like I wasn't smart enough to be his dad.

What could I possibly teach him? These are the questions I constantly asked myself. And as a father, this is when I made my biggest mistake. You see, I thought that just because Anthony was my son, he would love the things I love, like sports, dancing or the same kind of music.

I found out pretty quickly that my blood wasn't the only blood running through his veins. At the time, I didn't understand it like I do now. But when he was little, I signed him up for T ball, when I should have signed him up for an art class. I was so excited, and he was so not! In my mind I thought that most sons dreamed about playing catch with their dads. At least that's what I did. But Anthony most likely would have a better time going to the dentist rather than having a catch with me. Anthony wasn't too fond of sports. It just wasn't his thing. He loved to draw and he had a spectacular eye and a steady hand. He also loved writing poetry. In fact, he had a poem published in a book of poetry when he was in the 3rd grade. Geography came to him naturally. In the 5th grade he won the National Geographic Geography Bee for his school. In 6th grade he mapped the entire world from memory.

You see, where I made my mistake was assuming that my son had the same dreams and desires I had as a kid. Then I tried to force them on him without even asking him. This was very difficult for me because of my selfish pride. I thought it was my job to mold my son into what he should be; or should I say, what I thought he should be. I never asked God what was His heart for my son. Nor did I ask my son what was it that he loved to do.

Like in football, sometimes the quarterbacks have to call an audible from the line of scrimmage. Let me explain that in English for all of you non-football fans. Sometimes in life while you are in the mist of your current plans you may have to make a change (call an audible) in order to keep the team moving in a positive direction. Now, sometimes when you change the plan without having time to sit down and think it through it really works. A winner is constantly in audible mode. A winner can identify the need to shift gears and change the plan that they already constructed, in order to have a better outcome for their future. Fathers, let this be a lesson for you to learn. Take time and identify what is it that your kids love to do. I've learned over the years to get behind whatever it is Anthony loves to do, even if it's not my thing. As fathers, we must lay a foundation of support. We must anchor those beams of confidence into the depths of our child's being. They need to know whether or not they can depend on our support at any level, whether they are the star of the team or the last alternate. I've learned so much from my boys. Each life lesson that I'm supposed to be teaching them, turns around to be a revelation passed on to me. Anthony will soon be entering into his freshman year of college. He's majoring in game art. I am so excited to able to watch him follow his dreams.

With Alex things where a bit different from Anthony. As a baby you could always count on seeing a bottle in Al's mouth and a ball in his hand. It didn't matter what kind of ball it was. If it bounced or rolled, if it was large or small, even if it was hard or soft, this did not matter to him. He had a fondness for balls. And he was animated about what each ball did. As he grew, so did his enthusiasm for balls, specifically baseballs. Maybe it was the white leather that drew Alex to a baseball. Maybe it was the unusual stitching wrapped around the ball. Or maybe it was just a flat out answer to prayer! Either way my youngest son had the desire I thought my oldest son would have.

Alex is what the young kids would call a "baller." He's just an athlete! No matter the sport, if it has a ball Alex would find a way to have fun. I don't think that there is a sport with a ball that Al couldn't play. He's just one of those kids that keeps amazing you on and off the field. Even though Al is a great athlete, I believe he was called to play baseball. Not just because he's great at it! Not just because he loves it! I believe it's his calling because he changes the atmosphere in the dugouts without even saying a word. However, Alex had a change of heart. Or should I say change of passion! Alex turned out to be an incredible musician. He taught himself how to play drums, electric guitar, acoustic guitar, and the bass guitar. He's also a remarkable song writer. Both of our boys are amazingly talented.

But, of course, I'm incredibly biased! But I've had an amazing revelation out of me being biased! You see, as much as I love my boys, and as proud of them as I am, I realized my job in life isn't to tell them what to do or how to live their life. It's to encourage them and guide them through life's obstacles, teaching them not to run from their problems, but to face their problems head on and conquer them, allowing my boys to know that they are victorious in life and that they can do all things in life, if they unlock the winner inside them, which is Christ's strength!

Tip for the Winner

A father's love is never too late to give to your kids. No matter how many time you may mess up!

Chapter 20

Be Healed!!

"O LORD my God, I called to you for help and you healed me."

~ Psalm 30:2 (NIV)

That first day at the conference we went to with Garry Oates, we saw dozens of people healed. It was incredible! There were people who were deaf that began to hear. There were a few people who could not walk, who got out of their wheelchairs and began to dance around. The look of joy covered their faces like a shaded tree on a hot, summer day. Tears of amazement ran down their faces, like raging water rapids heading for a cliff. It was truly something to see. The next day I was the first in line for prayer. I just knew I was going to be healed. I remembered what that lady in the store told me years ago about being healed. I thought this was that day. As Garry Oats prayed for me, my body went completely south. I literally had no control over it. Now, normally when people get prayer, they tend to fall backwards. But for me I was an exception to that rule. I guess I didn't get the memo! I ended up falling forward and landed all of my 305 lbs. on top of the man. I had no control over my body, and I just rag-dolled him! I'm sure he had to lay hands on his own back after that! As I got up with great anticipation someone shoved a mic in my face and asked, "Are you healed?" Unfortunately I was not. In fact, I was in more pain than I was when I first came in to the meeting. Of course, I was very disappointed, but I would not give up! I would not quit! I would not stop believing in what was told to me. I knew that God was going to heal me.

A few weeks after we had gotten back from the conference, Tammy came across this place they call" healing rooms." Basically, all it was, was a group of Christians that got together in the basement of the church to pray for the sick. As we drove to the church, I did not know what to expect. For me, it was kind of different because it wasn't a church service. Basically, it was three of the kindest people I had ever met. There were two sweet, gentle and compassionate older ladies in there 70's and one middle-aged man in his 50's. The man began to interview me by asking me a series of questions. I don't recall the majority of the questions. However, one question he asked me I could never forget. He asked me did I forgive everyone that had to do with my accident: Did I forgive my employer who made it seem as if I was lying about the accident; Did I forgive the insurance company that stopped paying my check for almost a year; And, did I forgive the insurance company doctor that said there was nothing wrong with me? I told him, "No, I had NOT forgiven them! I was angry at them for what they put my family through." He looked at me and said, "As long as you have anger and bitterness in your heart, you will stay in their prison. Anger wants to steal your joy, and bitterness wants to rob your future! You must forgive in order to be released from that prison." I told him that I didn't want to stay in their prison anymore. So I asked God to forgive me for my anger towards them. And for him to bless them! After that, the friendly, warm-hearted man gently touched my arm and said, "Be healed in Jesus name!" Immediately I was consumed by a burst of fire shooting down my arm! My fingers began to straighten up, and I was able to move my arm! I was instantly healed! The pain left and I was in shocked! Without delay, the water rapids burst from my eyes, and I fell to my knees with gratefulness in my heart and joy on my face. I was completely overwhelmed with love. I was surrounded and wrapped up with liquid love as if I was submerged in an ocean of love. However, this ocean did not drown me--It saved and transformed my life forever!! I went back to my doctor and he told me that this was impossible. He said I could not be healed because there was no cure for this disease. I told him I felt no more pain, and I could move my arm on my own. He said that it was just in remission and that I still had the disease. Due to his diagnosis, I ended up getting a hefty settlement. I guess that lady who told me I would be healed *and* get a hefty settlement wasn't so crazy after all!

After my healing, the real journey began. I started to see and experience incredible, supernatural occurrences. These experiences propelled us into unimaginable encounters, miracles and blessings. The power inside of me was unlocked! And that power is called the Holy Spirit! That same warrior inside of me started to rise up to conquer my dreams!!! That same warrior can be inside of you and unlocked. All you have to do is ask Jesus to come in and take over your heart! When you surrender to Him, in no time, you'll begin to think like a winner, and unlock the power inside of you!

There are so many more stories to share of this life journey that we are on. Please know that this is not an ending to the story, but a pause! Please look out for another project in phase 2 of our "Think Like a Winner" series. Please join with us by pressing play on our next project when it is released! Thank You So Much!

Made in the USA
Columbia, SC
31 October 2017